CW00952790

TODMORDEN
EXTRAORDINARY

- exploring a Pennine mill town

My thanks for help in pushing this book over the line, to:

Joanne Blaker, Tina Blaker, Barry Cook, Sandra Evans, Jon Gower, Sally Hinton, Graham Joyce, Dave Marshall, Joan Marshall, *Radcliffe & Maconie* on *BBC6 Music*, Penny Nicholson, Robinwood Activity Centre, Eleanor Saunders, Pam Warhurst.

Published in 2019 by the author:
Jim Saunders, Burford House, Knighton, Powys.
www.jimsaunders.co.uk

ISBN 978-1-5272-4500-6

Printed and bound in Wales by Gomer Press
www.gomerprinting.co.uk

<u>Front cover:</u> *Mill chimney at Pudsey, Cornholme, photographed on 35mm Ilford Pan F, in 1987. (see p.75).*

<u>Back cover:</u> *The apse, Todmorden Town Hall, also on Pan F in 1987 (see p.42).*

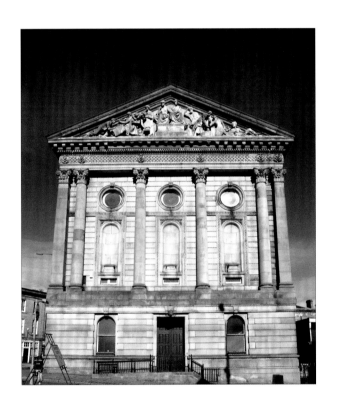

TODMORDEN
EXTRAORDINARY

- exploring a Pennine mill town

by Jim Saunders

▲ On the Long Causeway

4 Contents

Contents

Hidden away deep in a steep-sided clough in the West
Yorkshire Pennines, surrounded by Wood Anemones and
Bluebells, is an extraordinary romantic ruin. Three storeys high,
stone built, and imposing, it has no road access and no
neighbours. The Ordnance Survey map marks it as "*Staups Mill*"
It must have been abandoned long ago, but why was it ever
built here, in this wild and difficult place? And why, then, left to
decay?

We will return to Staups Mill, but first let me introduce you
to Todmorden.

◄ *Back-to-backs, Todmorden, 1973, photographed on 120 roll film*

The camera I used back then, my dad's Voigtlander Bessa 66 ►

Introduction: Todmorden and me.

It was 1973 when I discovered Todmorden. An innocent abroad from the soft South of England, I had never seen anything like it, and it made a big impression. Everything about it seemed extraordinary. For one thing I had never seen real back-to-backs before. Worse than that, like many southerners, I did not even know what true back-to-backs were. I had grown up in Sutton Avenue, surrounded by leafy suburbia, while here in Todmorden people lived in gritstone terraces on Industrial Street surrounded by wild and windy moors.

Back then I had no idea that 10 years later I would be living in this archetypal northern mill town. I only lived here for four years but those four years too left their mark, so that decades later I still think, and dream, a lot about Todmorden.

It was not only the place, I will grant you. In 1983, the year I moved to Todmorden, both of my parents-in-law died, prematurely, and my son was born. Two years later my daughter arrived while we still lived in Todmorden. And there was the big Edwardian gritstone house, riddled with damp and dry rot, which we bought and brought back to health. It was a busy time.

But enough about me, you want to know about Todmorden.

Todmorden YW [*Tottermerden, Totmardene*
1246 Ass, *Todmarden* c1300 WhC]. '*Totta's
boundary valley.*' Second el. OE (ge) mær-
denu.

Ekwall, *English Place-names*

The
Landscape of
Todmorden

◄ *Gritstone field walls at Mankinholes*

"Where the surface rock is Millstone Grit ... the characteristic landscape is wild, sweeping moorland, frequently covered with peat."

Alec Clifton-Taylor, *The Pattern of English Building*

If you asked me to describe the landscape around Slough, where I grew up, I'd be tempted to say "*There isn't any*". Todmorden, on the other hand, has loads of landscape. It's a very distinctive landscape too, and many of its typical features can be seen in this view south across the Calder Valley from Blackshawhead.

There's Millstone Grit for a start. The field walls are made of it, the farmhouse is built of it, even the farmhouse roof is covered with slabs of it. Around Stoodley Pike, on the far horizon, the moorland is dotted with dark outcrops and boulders of more Millstone Grit. And the Pike itself is built of Millstone Grit.

Stoodley Pike is the local landmark. Its unmistakeable outline is visible from all the surrounding hills, and from many parts of the town too. It stands on Langfield Common, an extensive area of moorland which is also designated a Site of Special Scientific Interest, for its wildlife. Todmorden is surrounded on all sides by these moors, with their characteristic buff shades created by great tussocks of Purple Moor Grass, interspersed with the paler Moor Mat Grass and clumps of dark rushes in the damp hillside cloughs. There are rushes too in the pasture in the foreground, a sign of poor, wet soils.

The fields just below Langfield Common, on the far side of the valley, are called intakes. Farmers have taken in land from the moor and enclosed it for pasture. These intakes are very much marginal land. At high altitude and on wet, acid soils they on the very edge of what can economically be farmed. The higher fields often revert to bog and rough grazing, a process which can be seen here.

What's a Clough?

When I showed a draft of this book to Welsh author and lecturer Jon Gower, he came back with a question which I had not expected: *"What's a clough?"* he said.

That made me realise just how local and distinctive the term, universally used around Todmorden, is. For there are cloughs galore in these here hills. There are tell-it-like-it-is cloughs: Black Clough, Coal Clough, Lead Mine Clough, Clay Roads Clough, and, yes, Clegg Clough. And there are cloughs with a bit of poetry: Rush Candle Clough, Daisy Bank Clough, Whinberry Clough, Light Hazzles Clough.

A quick tour of the Todmorden area on the Ordnance Survey Explorer map soon reveals several more words which, to me, instantly conjure up the South Pennine landscape: Intake, Moss, Bents, Delphs, Moor, Withens, Hey, Gate (Limers Gate), Royd, Slack, Wham. Every one of them is an integral part of the landscape.

Then, on the moors north from Todmorden, toward Widdop and Gorple Reservoirs, there are more Stones than you can shake a stick at: Hare Stones, Hawk's Stones, Dove Stones, Wolf Stones, Clattering Stones, Resting Stones, Boggart Stones, Bride Stones, Golden Stones, Grey Stones, and even a Round Stone. *"Stone me!"*, as my dad used to say.

More on cloughs later.

Another archetypal South Pennine scene. A handsome gritstone farmhouse, sheltered by a few broadleaved trees, and surrounded by green fields between dry stone walls, with moorland beyond.

This is Greenhurst Hey Farm, on the hillside just north of Todmorden.

◄◄ *A view across Todmorden from Great Rock. The town itself is there, but hidden from view in the valley bottom. The tower of Cross Stone church is just visible.*

Old Royd ►

20 The Landscape of Todmorden

Pennine Ways

If you want to get out on foot and explore the landscape of Todmorden for yourself, you will find that walkers are quite well provided for hereabouts. History has left the hills and cloughs around the town with an unusually dense network of local footpaths (see *The Buildings of Todmorden, p.27*), but several long-distance routes have also been laid onto this network.

Best known of these must be the Pennine Way, which was opened in 1965 and follows the high ground for 268 miles, between Edale, in the Peak District, and Kirk Yetholm, in the Cheviot Hills. It overlooks Todmorden from Stoodley Pike and crosses the Halifax Road at Callis Bridge, three miles down the Calder Valley. The more recent Pennine Bridleway passes through Lumbutts and Mankinholes, and the Calderdale Way circles the hills above the town.

There are much older long-distance routes too. Just below the watershed between Todmorden and Bacup the Ordnance Survey map shows "*Limers gate*". *Gate* or *gata* is an Old Norse word for a road or street, and before the days of railways, canals, or even turnpike roads, this track would have been used to transport the lime which was spread on the acid Pennine fields to make them more fertile. Above Cornholme the Long Causeway is believed to have been a Roman Road. Striding forth straight across moor and clough it certainly looks the part.

Cornholme, by the way, also has Norse roots, *holme/holmr* is Old Norse, and modern Norwegian, for an islet.

Sandra Evans, Dairy Farmer

Sandra Evans was having a good day when I went to meet her at Pextenement Farm, below Great Rock. Not because of me, you understand, but because her cheese had just won three awards at the Great Yorkshire Show, including overall Best Organic Product, and then, that very morning, she had taken delivery of a brand-new calf.

Sandra uses her former husband's surname, but she was born a Sutcliffe, and she is proper Yorkshire. Grandpa Sutcliffe came from Blackshawhead to take on the tenancy of Pextenemant in 1926, Grandma Sutcliffe was from Lumbutts, and one of Sandra's ancestors even worked on the building of Stoodley Pike. Sandra herself was born at neighbouring Higher East Lee farm and now runs Pextenement with her brother Alan, producing organic dairy products from 65 milking cows. Sandra's partner, Carl, started making cheese on the farm about ten years ago, but, she says, it did take a while to get the hang of it. Clearly they have it sorted now though. Milk from Pextenement also goes to the organic co-operative Omsco, and some of this is used to make cheese for export to the USA.

I asked Sandra which county Todmorden belongs to. *"Yorkshire,"* she said, without hesitation. At school she was taught that Town Hall (p.42) was deliberately built across the county boundary, in an attempt to unite the Yorkshire and Lancashire sides of the town.

I went away with one of Sandra's award-winning Devil's Rock cheeses. It was very good indeed.

The Buildings of Todmorden

◀ *Lumbutts Methodist Church (in 1983)*

"The weaver was continually pressing upon the spinner. The processes of spinning and weaving were generally performed in the same cottage, but the weaver's own family could not supply him with a sufficient quantity of weft, and he had with much pains to collect it from neighbouring spinsters. Thus his time was wasted, and he was often subjected to high demands for an article, on which, as the demand exceeded the supply, the seller could put her own price."

Edward Baines (1835), on the days before mechanisation.

Sixteen miles from Manchester, and equidistant between Burnley, Rochdale and Halifax, Todmorden is administratively in Yorkshire. Culturally though, it has always seemed to me to belong to Lancashire. As Sandra Evans observed, there was a time when the county boundary actually went through the Town Hall, and to this day the town has a Lancashire postal address. But, most importantly of all, present-day Todmorden was built on that most Lancashire of industries: cotton. It is, or was, an archetypal Lancashire cotton mill town.

Although there was a settlement here long before cotton started to be imported and manufactured, present-day Todmorden owes its size and shape to cotton, and to the industrial revolution of the 18th and 19th centuries. But there was a textile industry in these hills in earlier years too.

Before cotton there was wool, and in the seventeenth and eighteenth centuries wool was spun and woven in gritstone cottages all over the hillsides of this part of the Pennines. The evidence of this, the original "cottage industry" is still easy to find. Look for houses with long rows of "weavers' windows" on the top floor. This is where the weaver had his loom, and the windows are high up and long, often the whole width of the house, to let in the maximum amount of natural light. The weavers lived below their looms and often farmed on a small scale as well. So each cottage had a few small fields alongside. Spinning too was done by hand, by "spinsters", usually women, often unmarried, working at home.

◀ *Early industrial landscape, at Jack Bridge, west of Heptonstall.*

"The association of small farming with manufacturing was common. Radcliffe, writing of the industrial conditions in 1770, says that the 'land in our township (Mellor) was occupied by between 50 and 60 farmers...and out of these ...there were only 6 or 7 who raised their rents directly from the produce of their farms; all the rest got their rent partly in some branch of trade, such as spinning and weaving woollen, linen or cotton. The cottagers were employed entirely in this matter except for a few weeks in the harvest.' "

Chapman, *The Lancashire Cotton Industry*, 1904.

The distinctive landscape produced by this pattern of industry is also still there to be seen, particularly on the sloping plateau to the north-east of Todmorden, around Blackshawhead and Heptonstall. The pioneer landscape historian Professor W.G.Hoskins described this area in his 1973 book *English Landscapes*, which accompanied a BBC TV series. He said:

"Perhaps the best of our early industrial landscapes, because it survives to this day in an easily recognisable form, is the countryside around Halifax and above all just west of Heptonstall, towards the high Lancashire border."

The principal mode of transport in these days was on foot or by packhorse. So all these scattered cottage workshops were connected by a dense network of paths and tracks. They are still there too. The Ordnance Survey Explorer Map of the South Pennines (No. OL21) shows a pattern of small fields, mainly walled in stone, dotted with cottages and criss-crossed by footpaths and bridleways. Many of these are now public rights-of-way, so the walker of today can literally follow in the footsteps of the weavers and traders of three and four hundred years ago.

◀ *Old packhorse road above Lumbutts.*

"Owing to the bad state of the roads, and the entire absence of inland navigation, goods could only be conveyed on pack-horses, with a gang of which the Manchester chapmen used occasionally make circuits of the principal towns and sell their goods to shop-keepers ...."

Edward Baines, on the Lancashire cotton industry of the 17th century.

As the industry became mechanised in the late 18th and early 19th centuries, production gradually moved into large water-powered "mills", a term almost certainly borrowed from the milling of flour which also often used water power. These new textile mills had to be where the water was, so they were built in the steep, narrow valleys where the rains from high Pennine moors gathered into streams big enough and fast enough to drive giant water wheels and power the new mill machinery. And yes, signs of these can still be seen. When I lived in Todmorden I was fascinated to discover that in almost any of the side valleys, or "cloughs", which fed the River Calder, the remains of old mills, mill ponds and waterworks could be found.

Typically water for a mill would be drawn from the stream some way up the valley. It would be diverted into an artificial channel (goit, goyt or leat) which had been built along the hillside, to run parallel to the stream. But while the natural watercourse tumbled on downhill the goit stayed level, following the contour of the valley side. So as stream and goit both progressed down the clough the difference in height between them steadily increased. By the time the mill was reached there would be a good "head" of water in the goit which would pour down over the waterwheel before meeting up again with its original course.

Back in the nineteen-eighties the first evidence of an old mill site that I would spot would be a horizontal bank running along a valley side. This marked the line of the old goit. Follow it up the valley and it would usually lead to the remains of a weir where the water had been diverted to feed the mill. Follow it in the other direction and, you never knew your luck, you might find the site of the mill itself.

◄ In Lumbutts Clough today

Because they were often very much out of the way and on very uneven ground many of these early works seem to have been simply abandoned and left slowly to decay, which is why we can sometimes still see their remains today. They were abandoned because of new technology: new power technology in the form of the steam engine, and new transport technology in the form of the Rochdale Canal. Steam engines were more powerful and more reliable than water wheels (they could work on through a dry summer), and the mills which they drove did not have to be built on an inaccessible site by a stream. But they did need coal, and the canal could supply this. So the next generation of textile workers moved downhill again, this time to work in the floor of the Calder Valley, close by the canal. In time though these mills too became obsolete, and many of them have disappeared in my lifetime.

So far so school-geography-textbook, but this really came to life for me the day I came across an old Ordnance Survey (OS) map of Todmorden.

The 1853 map of Lumbutts Clough, at 1:10,560 scale, names no fewer than six mills set in the clough. Starting at the hamlet of Lumbutts and descending to the River Calder they are marked as Lumbutts Mill (cotton), Jumb Mill (cotton), Causeway Mill (cotton), Causeway Wood Mill (cotton), Old Royd Mill (cotton), and Woodhouse Mill (cotton). Fifty four years later,

on a map dated 1907, Causeway Mill, and Causeway Wood Mill are not mentioned, while Old Royd Mill is shown as "disused".

I photographed Woodhouse Mill in 1976, and again in 2013. My earlier picture shows a tall, soot-blackened gritstone mill, complete with the traditional mill chimney. So this had been a steam-powered mill. By 2013 it had been cleaned and converted to house what looked to be some rather upmarket flats, but the chimney was still there, and now I noticed that the mill stands right on the bank of the Rochdale Canal. In fact the canal laps against its northern wall, and a column of tall narrow windows shows where once there would have been doors for the loading and unloading of goods to and from boats below.

An 1852 Town Plan shows the canal running westward from Woodhouse Mill to Todmorden town centre. There are open fields all the way from Kilnhurst Bridge to Baltimore Bridge. But by 1907 the following have appeared: Sandholme Mill (cotton), Derdale Mill (cotton), Der Street Mill (cotton), Anchor Mill (cotton), Hope Street Mill (cotton), Canal Street Works Mill (machinery & cotton), and Albion Mill (cotton).

Here was clear documentary evidence of the evolution of the cotton industry and its impact on Todmorden's built environment.

▲ *Woodhouse Mill, 1976*

Woodhouse Mill, 2013 ▲

Millstone Grit

We have established that Todmorden is a cotton town, but just as essential to its character is Millstone Grit. It is Millstone Grit that makes the Pennine hills which cradle the town, it is Millstone Grit that gives the Pennine moors their acid soils, it is Millstone Grit that makes the field walls surrounding the moors and it's Millstone Grit which built the streets of the town.

So what is this Millstone Grit? Also known as gritstone, it is, geologically speaking, a sandstone. That is to say that it is a stone made of grains of sand which are held together by a kind of glue called the matrix. Not all sandstones are good for building, some rapidly crumble away when exposed to wind and weather, but not Millstone Grit. In *The Pattern of English Building* architectural historian Alec Clifton-Taylor tells us that it is the matrix which makes the difference. It is rich in silica, which makes for a hard-wearing sandstone resistant both to weather and air pollution. Ideally suited to a Pennine mill town then.

Clifton Taylor also says of Millstone Grit:

> *"Its very name is rooted in history, for when water-power operated the little water mills of the Pennine villages it was from this tough, gritty sandstone that they fashioned the millstones."*

Once the Clean Air Acts of the 1960's created Smokeless Zones people took to cleaning old stone buildings, sometimes with spectacular results, as at London's Natural History Museum. And stone cleaning came to Todmorden too. There were dark mutterings in some quarters about prettyifying our industrial heritage, and when some houses in a terrace were cleaned and others were not, the results could look a little odd.

◄ *The apse, with Corinthian columns, at the rear of the Town Hall. A classical feature, originating in Roman times, as part of a basilica, the apse was later adapted to form the chancel in Christian churches, says John Henry Parker in his* Gothic Architecture *of 1881.*

The Town Hall

Probably Todmorden's most notable and distinguished building is the Town Hall, one reason being that you can't really miss it. Right in the centre of town, facing the roundabout where the roads from Rochdale, Burnley and Halifax meet, it is an imposing work of Victorian architecture in the Classical (ancient Greek/Roman) style.

In their book *Victorian Architecture* Roger Dixon and Stefan Muthesius write:

"*In 1860-75 the comparatively small Yorkshire town of Todmorden was able to build a magnificent town hall thanks to a gift of £40,000 by the local industrialist Samuel Fielden and his family. It is a simplified version of St. George's Hall [Liverpool], a plain rectangle with an apse at one end, surrounded by a giant attached Corinthian order. The designer was John Gibson, whom we have met as the architect of Renaissance banks.*"

Historic England have given the Town Hall a Grade 1 listing, meaning that it has the highest level of protection for a historic building, on a par with York Minster. They describe it as

"*... a building of concentrated richness and great assurance unusual in this style at that period. One of the finest town halls in West Yorkshire.*"

The Town Hall frontage ▶

The Town Hall pediment
Can you see a blacksmith, a shepherd, a woman carrying a basket of shuttles, another with a tray of bobbins, a third reaping corn, barefoot, and an accountant? And did you notice that, of the workers depicted here, four are women and four men, whilst the counties of Lancashire and Yorkshire seem to be represented by ladies of leisure?

"This helps to produce the impression of a rugged and purposeful architecture, not much concerned with the graces of ornamental enrichment..."

Alec Clifton-Taylor on Millstone Grit.

Stoodley Pike

You could say that Stoodley Pike epitomises all that is gritty and masculine about Todmorden's landscape. A massive gritsone column right on top of the Pennines, 400 metres (1,300 ft) above sea level, there is nothing gentle about it. Its distinctive silhouette can be seen for many miles in every direction, while close up it is heavy, hard, dark, forbidding even. A carved stone tablet on the side of the pike itself records its history as follows:

> STOODLEY PIKE A PEACE MONUMENT ERECTED
> BY PUBLIC SUBSCRIPTION COMMENCED IN 1814
> TO COMMEMORATE THE SURRENDER OF PARIS
> TO THE ALLIES AND FINISHED AFTER THE BATTLE
> OF WATERLOO WHEN PEACE WAS ESTABLISHED
> IN 1815. BY A STRANGE COINCIDENCE THE PIKE
> FELL ON THE DAY RUSSIAN AMBASSADOR LEFT
> LONDON BEFORE THE DECLARATION OF WAR
> WITH RUSSIA IN 1853 *REBUILT WHEN PEACE WAS
> RESTORED IN 1856 REPAIRED AND LIGHTNING
> CONDUCTOR 1889

The cotton industry being completely dependent on international trade, Todmorden's economy was particularly vulnerable in times of war. Worse was to come after Stoodley Pike was rebuilt, when the American Civil War of the 1860's created the infamous Cotton Famine.

Springside Branch, Todmorden Industrial and Co-operative Society Limited

I photographed this extraordinary building in 1973 (opposite, with my touring bike) and again in 1976 (above). On the second occasion a notice told me that it had been scheduled for demolition, and, sure enough, when I moved to Todmorden in 1983 it had gone.

Sandwiched between the Halifax Road and the River Calder, about one mile east of the town centre, it fronted both. The suspended walkway in the 1973 picture led to the front, yes, front, doors of eight houses which seemingly had no other access. Note the letterbox and house number on the door at top left of 1976 picture. Also, to the right, the stone structure overhanging the river, which appears to be an outside privy.

My title comes from a plaque I found on the Halifax Road side of the building, which also displayed the date 1869. Clear evidence that land for housing was in short supply in mid nineteenth-century Todmorden.

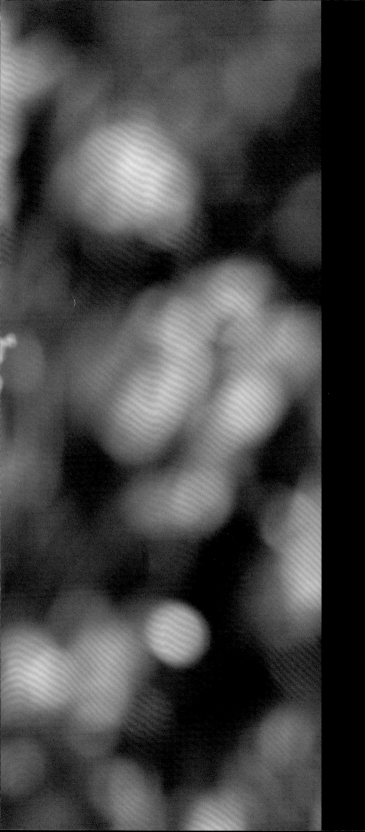

The Flora of Todmorden

◀ *Bilberry flowers above Cornholme*

For botanists and gardeners the key word about the flora of Todmorden is "acid". Another is of course "wet". The gritstones and shales of which Todmorden's landscape is formed are acid, so the soils which form on them are acid too, and only plants which can tolerate acid conditions thrive. Not for Todmorden the orchid-rich limestone flora of the Derbyshire Peak District or Dales of North Yorkshire.

Two of the classic acid-tolerant plants of the Pennine moors around Todmorden are the purple Heather, *Calluna vulgaris*, and the Bilberry, *Vaccinium myrtillus*. They will commonly be found growing on peat, another thing for which the Pennines (and the Pennine Way), are famous. This is where "wet" comes in. Peat soils form in places where there is high rainfall and/or poor drainage, and they are made up of the blackened remains of partly decomposed plants. Peat forms because waterlogging prevents the normal processes of decomposition. As well as Heather and Bilberry the easily-spotted Cotton Grasses, *Eriophorum vaginatum* and *Eriophorum angustifolium* (strictly speaking not true grasses, but sedges), and the thick spongy *Sphagnum* Moss will be found growing in the boggier parts of the moors.

Another characteristic habitat of the Todmorden area is the damp, shady woodland of the deep Pennine cloughs. There I went looking for Ramsons, *Allium ursinum*, often called "Wild Garlic" and Wood Sorrel, *Oxalis acetosella*. I found also Wood Anemone, *Anemone nemorosa* and Great Wood Rush, *Luzula sylvatica*.

Ramsons in Lumbutts Clough

Ramsons (Allium ursinum) is one of my favourite plants. Sometimes called Wild Garlic its leaves smell strongly of onions, to which it is related. Typically it grows in damp shady places, often alongside streams, and it flowers in Spring. One of my abiding memories of living in Todmorden is of walking from our house in Kilnhurst through this carpet of Ramsons on our way to Stoodley Pike. I went back in 2010 to see if I could capture the memory in a photograph. The Ramsons was still there but I had missed its flowering season. In 2016 I tried again and carefully calculated when would be the best time to go. But it was 15th May 2018 when I found this, the picture I really wanted for a double-page spread. ▶▶

▲ Bog Asphodel grows, as the name suggests, on wet, acid, soils. It is a pretty enough plant, but it is its Latin name which fascinates me: *Narthecium ossifragum*. *Ossifragum*, "fragile bones" or "bone breaker", refers to the effect that these acid soils, low in bone-building calcium, have on grazing livestock. There is no shortage of wet, acid soils on the hills around Todmorden, and Joshua Holden, writing in 1912, records Bog Asphodel as growing locally. Have you seen it? I have not yet. I took this picture in Mid Wales.

Also in Lumbutts Clough, right on the roadside, I found these perky little Wood Sorrel flowers ▶

Rush Candle Clough

Rush Candle Clough: it's an evocative name, but what does it mean? Luckily, if you know where to look, the information is out there. Writing in November 1755 the Reverend Gilbert White gives a detailed description of how, in the days before electric, or even gas, lighting, people made candles to light their homes from wild rushes.

White recommends the "*common soft rush*", *Juncus conglomeratus*, for the job. So, I thought, "*I must look into this. I wonder if Juncus conglomeratus still grows in Rush Candle Clough*".

Gilbert White by candle light ▶

LETTER XXVI.

TO THE SAME.

SELBORNE, *Nov. 1st, 1775.*

tædæ pingues, hic plurimus ignis
assidua postes fuligine nigri."

I make no apology for troubling you on a very simple piece of domestic satisfied that you think nothing attention that you tends to utility: the the use of rushes instead of candles, ware prevails in many districts I know there are countries also in, and as I have considered the tree of exactness, I shall proceed and leave you to judge of the

f rush for this purpose seems to atus, or common soft rush, which moist pastures, by the sides of ges. These rushes are in best summer; but may be gathered. se well, quite on to autumn. d that the largest and longest rs, women and children, make e and prepare them. As soon be flung into water, and kept will dry and shrink, and the a person would find it no of its peel or rind, so as to ven rib from top to bottom but this like other feats, to children; and we have ind, performing this busi- d seldom failing to strip rity. When these *junci* ust lie out on the grass ew for some nights, and

dipping these rushes in

the scalding fat or grea attained by practice. The Hampshire labourer obtains all her fat to be for she saves the scummings of her bacon-pot for this use; and, if the grease abounds with salt, she causes the salt to precipitate to the bottom, by setting the scummings in a warm oven. Where hogs are not much in use, and especially by the sea-side, the coarser animal-oils will come very cheap. A pound of common grease may be procured for four-pence, and about six pounds of grease will dip a pound of rushes, and one pound of rushes may be bought for one shilling; so that a pound of rushes, medicated and ready for use; will cost three shillings. If men that keep bees will mix a little wax with the grease, it will give it a con- sistency, and render it more cleanly, and make the rushes burn longer; mutton-suet would have the same effect.

A good rush, which measured in length two feet four inches and an half, being minuted, burnt only three minutes short of an hour; and a rush of still greater length has been known to burn one hour and a quarter. These rushes give a good clear light. Watch-lights (coated with tallow), it is true, shed a dismal one, "darkness visible"; but then the wicks of those have two ribs of the rind, or peel, to support the pith, while the wick of the dipped rush has but one. The two ribs are intended to impede the progress of the flame and make the candle last.

In a pound of dry rushes, avoirdupois, which I caused to be weighed and numbered, we found upwards of one thousand six hundred individuals. Now suppose each of these burns, one with another, only half an hour, then a poor man will purchase eight hundred hours of light, a time exceeding thirty-three entire days, for three shillings. According to this account each rush, before dipping, costs of a farthing, and afterwards. Thus a poor family will enjoy five and a half hours of comfortable light for a farthing. An error housekeeper assures me th

And that is how I came to be parking my car at Stiperden Bar, above the Long Causeway, one fine October day, and setting off uphill, following the present-day County Boundary between Yorkshire and Lancashire. This is Stiperden Moor, classic acid Pennine moorland with bilberry and heather growing on black peat. It is part of the South Pennine Moors Site of Special Scientific Interest (SSSI) and is also open to public access, so in theory one can wander at will. But it is also rough, tussocky terrain, where it would be easy to twist an ankle, so it is much easier to follow one of the well-worn informal paths.

At Wolf Stones I paused, perched, and soaked up the sun, while I ate my lunch, with a fine view south across successive ridges and valleys, each a little more blue than the one before. Then, tearing myself away, I pressed on to the summit Trig Point* on Hoof Stones Height, 479 metres above sea level.

The hazards of finding your way in bad weather on the high Pennine moors are well known, but I have to tell you, even on a clear, sunny, autumn day it is not a straightforward matter.

*Ordnance Survey Triangulation Pillar, originally used for map making.

▲ *Wolf Stones..*

  ..and the view south ▶

According to the map if I headed east-north-east from the trig point I would gradually descend into Rush Candle Clough, where I would find a stream. So I did that, and sure enough before long I found myself in a boggy hollow. I worked my way down this, eyes peeled for rushes and in due course I found some. But were they the right rushes? Were they White's *Juncus conglomeratus*? Hoping for the best, and not entirely sure that I was in Rush Candle Clough anyway, I photographed them.

Back at base I seek reassurance in my library. Yes, this looks like the *Juncus conglomeratus* which another Reverend gentleman, W. Keble Martin illustrates in his *New Concise British Flora* of 1965. But he gives the the English name of Compact Rush, whilst he gives Soft Rush the scientific name *Juncus effusus*. Then Richard Mabey, in his *Flora Britannica*, also referring to Gilbert White, suggests *Juncus effusus* as the real thing. He offers a photo. I look at his photo, I look at my photo, and I am none the wiser.

So I am not at all sure that I answered the question, but I did at least have an excellent afternoon out.

▲ *Navigate this*

◄ *In Rush Candle Clough?*

On
Bacup
Road

◄ *I did find Wood Sorrel*

..an embankment running horizontally along the hillside ►

On Bacup Road

It was in pursuit of Ramsons and Wood Sorrel that I set off up the Bacup road, but I found more than I expected.

First I came upon Gorpley Clough Nature Reserve, with a small car park, where a useful information board told me all about the geology of the site. There I did find Wood Sorrel too, and some small waterfalls on the Midgelden Brook. Having photographed these I drove on, and suddenly my eye was caught by an embankment running horizontally along the hillside opposite the road. This looked very much like an archetypal Pennine mill goit. And sure enough, as I continued up the valley the embankment and the brook drew level, and as they met I found an old weir, with sluice gear, rusting, but intact.

But by now it was getting late, and the sun was soon going to disappear behind the hills, so I resolved to come back next morning, and headed back down to Gauxholme. Before I got there though I was brought up short again, this time by Stoneswood Mill, right by the road and beautifully lit by the evening sun against a clear blue sky.

....sure enough, as I continued up the valley the embankment and the Brook drew ▶
level and as they met I found an old weir, with sluice gear rusting but intact.

▲ ..*an exposed concrete pipe, running in the channel..*

▲ .... *a mysterious vertical concrete cylinder*

The unmistakeable tall, narrow, stone ruins of a waterwheel pit. ▶

Next morning it was fine again, and back at the Nature Reserve Car Park I started to follow the Reserve Trail. This almost immediately brought me to another part of the goit, which proved to be very interesting indeed. As I walked along it, toward the weir, I came across an exposed concrete pipe running in the channel, then, further along, a mysterious vertical concrete cylinder rising out of it. The material was interesting. Evidently the goit had been in use, for something, in the era of concrete, probably after the second World War. I retraced my steps, climbed over a recently fallen tree, and found another concrete column, this time one which had been extended with few courses of stone at the top. Around it was what might once have been a small header pond, but down in the clough, below this, was some very interesting-looking masonry.

A short scramble later I was looking up at the unmistakeable tall, narrow, stone ruins of a waterwheel pit. So now I had almost the whole set: weir, goit, waterwheel pit. Only the mill was missing, and though there was small two-storey building at the roadside I doubted that this was it.

Stoneswood Mill

Having photographed Stoneswood Mill on my return from Gorpley Clough, I searched on line for "Thistle Brand Pickers" to see what I could learn. Somewhat surprisingly the only reference which this produced was to set of vintage playing cards for sale on e-bay. The cards bore the legend "Walton's Thistle Brand pickers, buffers and leathers". Clearly the seller did not know any more than I did, since his description of the item included the following:

> "An unusual duty sealed deck advertising a Scottish company I think as the item advertised is Thistle Brand. I do not know what pickers, buffers & leathers refers to... dated early 1940's early 50's."

Mapwork enabled me to find the name of the mill though, and from that I established that it was now owned by P&M Services of Rochdale, manufacturers of Printed Circuit boards. Their own website gives a short history on the mill and reveals that it was once owned by the Fieldens (p.98).

So, pickers? A picker is part of a loom, and it's function was to propel the shuttle through the warp, although there was also a picking machine which cleaned the raw cotton before it was spun. So at Stoneswood Mill, as in the bobbin mills of Cornholme (coming up), they made components for weaving machinery, rather than weaving cotton itself.

I passed on the e-bay ad to Roger Unwin of P&M Services, by the way, and he bought the cards.

Cornh

◄ Shore

Todmorden is extraordinary, but Cornholme is even more so. It is a pocket Todmorden, a Pennine mill town stripped of all but the essentials and wedged into the bottom of a valley so narrow and so steep you have to wonder who ever thought it could work. But work is one thing it certainly did: at least five mills once clustered in the valley bottom where Redwater Clough meets the infant River Calder.

In this view of Cornholme from above the houses in the foreground are true back-to-backs: each terrace contains two rows of houses, built back-to-back. Each side of each terrace therefore has a row of front doors facing on to a street. There are no back doors or back windows. These houses appeared on the Ordnance Survey map between 1848 and 1894. On the far side of the main road the three terraces nearest the church came later. They have back yards, albeit very small ones, and are therefore not true back-to-backs. These streets, the church and the red brick building, which was a Sunday School, appear for the first time on the 1911 map. Previously the Vale Bobbin Mill had stood there.

Cornholme from above ▶

If you come into Cornholme from Todmorden look out for a minor road to the right, signposted to Shore. It is worth exploring. It's no Alpine pass, but it climbs steeply out of the valley, twisting this way and that, so that, if driving, you have little opportunity to look at the view. If cycling, on the other hand, you may only too pleased to stop and do so. When I was there in May 2010 they were still demolishing a mill close by the junction with the main road. Almost immediately the road forked and narrowed. The right fork took me uphill past an elegant little Victorian terrace of half-a-dozen houses, with iron railings going up the slope in steps. I remembered this terrace, I had photographed it back in the eighties. Then, on the left, a red brick mill chimney rose up out of nowhere.

As the buildings rapidly thin out there is a sharp bend to the left and a stile in the fence on the right. Hop over this, walk a few yards into the field and you will find yourself looking at Cornholme from above. Across to your right is Frost Holme Mill, pictured opposite. Note the glass roofs of the old weaving sheds behind and to the left of the mill. Neither the mill nor the houses in the foreground appear on the Ordnance Survey map of 1848, when the site was shown as Frost Hole. Freezing air naturally settles in the bottoms of these steep-sided Pennine valleys, which see very little, if any, sun in winter.

▲ *An elegant little Victorian Terrace, 1986*

Frost Holme Mill 2010　　　　　　▶

▲ Cornholme, 1976

".. a red brick mill chimney rose up out of nowhere." ▶

This is Dawk Hole, Pudsey, Cornholme, in June 2010. The chimney rose (it has now gone) from the site of the former Glen Dye Works. According to the 1853 Ordnance Survey map the dye works had previously been the Pudsey Bobbin Mill. Nineteenth century maps show at least four bobbin mills wedged cheek-by-jowl into the valley bottoms in Cornholme and Pudsey: Pudsey Mill, Springwood Mill, Vale Mill and Cornholme Mill. Evidently Cornholme was big in bobbins.

Here (left) is Victoria Street, Cornholme, photographed in 2010. In the foreground the ubiquitous modern concrete paviours, but the main part of the street is still of flat gritstone setts (not cobbles, which are different) between gritstone houses. The far end of the terrace has been stone-cleaned. Beyond this a retaining wall supports the railway line, above which the valley side rises steeply, with typical acid heathland vegetation of heather and silver birch. This close juxtaposition of tightly-packed terraced streets and relatively wild countryside is characteristic of the area. I found quite it quite extraordinary when I first came here as a wide-eyed Southerner in the 1970's.

The only external wall which a true back-to-back has, is its street frontage. So when these houses had bathrooms installed that was where the soil pipes had to go, as seen here. There is no back yard to dry washing either, so traditionally it was, often still is, hung across the street, and nowhere to put a dustbin, also seen here.

▲ *Big in bobbins, Cornholme 2016*

◀ *Victoria Street Cornholme*

Joan Marshall

Joan Marshall, Millworker, retired.

Joan Marshall is a Lancashire lass, and not really local. She's from Bacup, where she worked in a munitions factory during World War II, making bullets. At 23 Joan moved to Todmorden to marry, and learned to weave at Stott's Mill on Halifax Road, before moving again, in 1948, to Cornholme. There, I was delighted to discover, she worked at Frost Holme Mill (p.79).

I asked Joan if she liked working in the mills. "*Not really,*" she said, "*it was not so good. I didn't like the noise.*" The pay was not very good either, and the weavers, mostly women, worked from 7.30 a.m. to 5.30 p.m. on weekdays, and then on Saturday mornings too. Joan lived just five minutes walk from the mill, as did most of her colleagues. At the end of the working day, she says, the main road was flooded with workers walking home.

I was introduced to Joan at Waterside Lodge Care Home by her son Dave, who grew up in Cornholme. Back then, he told me, there had been a bank, a butcher, a baker, and a chemist. It was a self-contained community. His sister told him that when she went from Cornholme to the Grammar School in Todmorden she felt very conscious that she spoke differently from the Todmorden pupils.

Like me, Dave, who now lives in Todmorden, thinks that the town is culturally Lancashire. It lacks the dourness and thrift of Yorkshire, he says. Ooh Sandra!

"With its humid atmosphere, its coal and its harbour, its climate rendering an indoor occupation desirable, and its general unsuitability for agriculture, Lancashire is marked out as a spot exceptionally well endowed for the prosecution of the cotton industry."

Sydney Chapman, 1904

Cotton

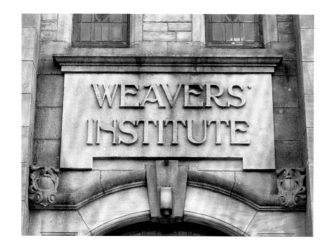

◄ *Art Nouveau lettering on the Weavers Institute in Burnley Road, opened 1914.*

Gossypium barbadense, Sea Island Cotton, ►
growing in Hawaii. (Photo courtesy of Forest and Kim Starr of starrenvironmental.com.)

"Up to the year 1760, the machines used in the cotton manufacture in England were nearly as simple as those of India; though the loom was more strongly and perfectly constructed and cards for combing the cotton had been adopted from the woollen manufacture...."

Edward Baines, 1835

So, it is all very well saying that Todmorden was a Lancashire cotton town, but what does this actually mean? Time to learn a little more. The history of the Lancashire cotton industry is a long and complex one, and has been the subject of many a learned tome, since as long ago as 1823. My bibliography on page 144 lists some of these, but here I will attempt only a much-reduced summary.

Cotton is a natural vegetable fibre, meaning that it comes from a plant, not an animal or an oil refinery. There are several different species of cotton, within the plant genus Gossypium. Writing in 1896, A.C True, of the United States Department of Agriculture, lists Gossypium arboreum, G. neglectum, G. brasiliense, G. herbaceum and G. barbadense as just a few examples.

Of Gossypium barbadense he says:

"This species is indigenous to the Lesser Antilles and probably to San Salvador, the Bahamas, Barbados, Guadaloupe, and other islands between 12° and 26° north latitude. By cultivation it has been extended throughout the West Indies, the maritime coast of the Southern States, Central America, Puerto Rico, Jamaica, etc., southern Spain, Algeria, the islands and coast of western tropical Africa, Egypt, Island of Bourbon, East Indies, Queensland, New South Wales, etc. It may be cultivated in any region adapted to the olive and near the sea, the principal requisite being a hot and humid atmosphere, but the results of acclimatization indicate that the humid atmosphere is not entirely necessary if irrigation be employed .. "

◀ Alfred Waterhouse's Manchester Town Hall of 1868-77, a masterpiece of Victorian Gothic Revival architecture. The great centre of the cotton industry, in the nineteenth century Manchester was nicknamed "Cottonopolis"

Busy bees: the floor mosaic at Manchester Town Hall ▶ celebrates the city's pre-eminence as a hive of industry. (My photos, taken and published with the permission of Manchester City Council.)

So cotton was not grown in Todmorden. Why then was it being manufactured here, in a place so far, and so different, from those where it was grown? Professor Sydney Chapman, of Manchester University, offers the following reasons in his 1904 book *The Lancashire Cotton Industry - A Study in Economic Development*:

> *"Lancashire presented to the cotton industry a group of natural advantages which, for the purposes of that industry, are unrivalled elsewhere. All the raw material for the manufacture must be imported; Liverpool offers almost unlimited harbourage. And the port being at hand the expansion of the industry by the development of an export trade was encouraged. Other things being equal, an industry will tend to export the more, the more it imports and the more its position has been determined by its needs as an importer. In addition to the port, Lancashire provided cheap coal, and, in addition to coal, an atmosphere just suited to the production of cotton goods. For spinning a damp climate is required, as otherwise the threads snap under the strain put upon them in the process of drawing and twisting. Dampness causes the fibres to cling together; and it has been found impossible to produce artificially and economically the peculiarities of the damp atmosphere. The spinning districts of Lancashire are so suitable because they lie on the slopes of hills facing west, upon which the damp breezes from the Atlantic discharge their moisture as they are driven to higher levels by the slope of the ground. With its humid atmosphere, its coal and its harbour, its climate rendering an indoor occupation desirable, and its general unsuitability for agriculture, Lancashire is marked out as a spot exceptionally well endowed for the prosecution of the cotton industry."*

Cotton wool, the product of the cotton plant, was being imported and processed in Lancashire as early as the mid 17th century. In 1641 Lewes Roberts reports that a range of cotton goods were being sent from Manchester to London to be sold, some for export. But was in late 1700's that the Lancashire cotton industry really began to take off, with a range of inventions which gradually mechanised the various processes involved in turning raw cotton into finished fabric.

Sydney Chapman lists these processes of cotton manufacture as: carding, drawing and roving, spinning, twining, weaving, bleaching, dyeing, printing and finishing. Of these, spinning, which elongates and twists cotton wool into a continous thread, was among the earliest to be mechanised. Historically, spinning had been done by hand, using a cleft stick called a distaff*. Later this was supersed by the familiar spinning wheel, but either method could only spin one length of thread at a time. The famous spinning jenny, invented by James Hargreaves, a Lancashire weaver, in the 1760's, increased the number of spindles, and therefore threads which could be worked, but was still hand-powered.

Output of spun yarn was greatly increased by the development of machines such Sir Richard Arkwright's Water Frame and, later, Samuel Crompton's Spinning Mule, but these were too heavy to work by hand and so required an external source of power: water. It was these machines which started the cotton industry's move from cottages dispersed about the hillsides around Todmorden to water-powered mills such as those in Lumbutts Clough. Working cotton thereby ceased to be a family business carried out at home and began the factory system, where employees operated machines belonging to a mill owner, their hours, rate of pay, and conditions of work now being in the control of their employer.

Spinning in particular seems to have been a Todmorden speciality, John Fielden, of Todmorden, is described by Victor Cohen as "*the largest cotton spinner in England*", and it is spinning which particularly benefits from the damp air, which helps to prevent yarn from breaking. But weaving became big business here as well. "*The spirit of improvement which had carried the spinning machine to so high a degree of perfection*," writes Edward Baines in 1835, "*was next directed to the weaving department, and did not rest til that operation, as well as spinning, was performed by machinery.*"

In 1787 the Rev. Edmund Cartwright invented a power-loom, which eventually superseded hand looms, though various technical difficulties meant it was not widely adopted until the 1830's. The period of development of power looms coincided with that of James Watt's steam engine, and Sydney Chapman reports that "*almost all the first power looms were driven by steam*" and that "*early in the nineteenth century the superiority of Watt's engines over water-power had been completely demonstrated and water mills ceased to be built*".

---

* From which genealogists get the term *distaff*, for the female line in a family tree.

▲ *Former mill chimney by the Rochdale Canal*

D. MILLS & CO.
SPRINGMAKERS
TEL: 817064

◄ *Closed down: Crossley's Shuttles*

Abandoned: Rock Nook Mill, Summit ►

"Amazing as is the progress which had taken place in the cotton manufacture prior to 1790 it would soon have found a check upon its further extension if a power more efficient than water had not been discovered to move the machinery. The building of mills in Lancashire must have ceased when all the available fall of the streams had been appropriated."

Edward Baines, 1835

It was also in the early 19th century (1804) that the Rochdale Canal arrived in Todmorden, bringing in imported raw cotton, and taking away finished goods for distribution and export. Water-power no longer being essential to running a mill, access to the canal, and the availability of relatively level land, gradually drew the industry to the valley bottom. (See *The Buildings of Todmorden*.)

And along with mechanised spinning and weaving came a range of satellite industries, supplying equipment to the mills, or products for the treatment of cotton goods.
So we have the bobbin mills and the Glen Dye Works in Cornholme, and, at Stoneswood Mill on Bacup Road, Thistle Brand Pickers. At Woodbottom Mill on Hollins Road, Crossley's Shuttles were manufactured and exported right up to 2006.

Crossley's did well to keep their business going so long though. The twentieth century saw the gradual decline of the UK's textile industries, in the face of competition from, ironically, developing countries such as India, which mechanised its own, much older, cotton industry. By the time I moved to Todmorden in 1983 abandoned mills had become a common sight on both sides of the Pennines and the demolition of mill chimneys regularly featured on television news. But on warm summer nights, with the windows open, we would still hear looms working, from our house in Kilnhurst.

21B   22   22A

- SAFETY -

◄ *Now you see them: the River Calder in Sowerby Bridge in 1975.*

Now you don't: the same view in 2019 ▼

Old textile mills continue to disappear on both sides of the Pennines. Down-river from Todmorden this view of the Calder in Sowerby Bridge has been transformed since I photographed it in 1975. As well as missing mills a dam just below the bridge has been breached, freeing the river but robbing me of those lovely reflections.

"The working men found exceedingly able and noble-hearted leaders, John Fielden, the wealthy cotton spinner of Todmorden in Lancashire, and Richard Oastler, a land agent of Yorkshire, who initiated the campaign.."
Victor Cohen on the Ten-Hour Day Campaign.

John Fielden MP

"*The sun has seldom shone over a better man than the late John Fielden*", wrote Robert Gammage in his *History of the Chartist Movement*, of 1854, and no description of Todmorden can be complete without reference to the Fieldens. Their family was a true cotton dynasty and very big indeed in Todmorden. They ran several cotton mills and have left the town three of its finest buildings: The Town Hall, the Unitarian Church and Dobroyd Castle, all now officially listed and protected by Historic England.

The John Fielden of whom Gammage wrote lived from 1784 to 1849 and was MP for Oldham. The title of his 1836 book: *The Curse of the Factory System* makes it clear that this was no ordinary Victorian industrialist. The Introduction to the 1969 (sic) Second Edition reports that Fielden worked in his father's mill for ten hours a day from the age of 10, and suggests that this experience "*exercised a major influence on his subsequent career.*" In Parliament Fielden introduced the Ten Hour Bill, which passed into law in 1847 and was intended to limit the length of the working day. He was also a Chartist: a supporter of The People's Charter and National Petition, which sought to reform Parliament and extend the right to vote to all men (though not women).

The first factories used water power and were therefore built near the becks and streams of the North of England (where mountain torrents are more plentiful than in the South) and in places isolated and remote from all towns. The owners found it difficult to obtain labour in these new " industrial bastilles," for men and women refused to enter. They were unable to endure the monotonous routine of the machine and they disliked the discipline and the regularity which factory life imposed. Even if poverty would have driven them to put up with these onerous conditions, there were no houses near these wind-swept factories where they could live.

So the owners looked round for other supplies of labour. Children were in every way ideal. They could be trained to endure the rigours of the industrial routine, they were helpless to resist any brutal overlooker, they were docile, their fingers were sufficiently deft to do the most delicate work ; but no self-respecting parent would permit his children to enter the factory, it was considered a disgrace. So the owners bought up pauper children from workhouses in London and other towns—in one contract thirteen to the dozen, of which one might be a cripple—to work in the mills. These pauper children were called apprentices, but in fact they were helpless child slaves ; for they were worked as hard as their little bodies would stand. They were housed together in a large Apprentice House, often little more than some large sheds which were erected near the factory. They slept two and three and sometimes four in one bed ; they were worked in shifts, so that as one set of child labourers was pulled out of bed to go to do their turn at the machine, another set replaced them in the still-warm bed.

Many worked for fourteen hours a day for six days a week and they were ill-clothed, ill-fed—the waifs of the Industrial storm then raging. Indeed, it was

◄ Victor Cohen, writing in 1932, on child labour in the cotton mills

Sculpture of African slave, Dobroyd Castle ►

"The yarn spun in Britain in 1833 would circle the globe 203,775 times, would reach the sun 51 times and would encircle the earth's orbit 8 ½ times. The wrought fabrics of cotton exported in one year would form a girdle for the globe, passing eleven times round the equator.

This manufacture furnishes nearly one half of the exports of British produce and manufacture; it supports one eleventh part of the population of Great Britain..."

Baines, *History of the Cotton Manufacture in Great Britain*, 1835

In the late eighteenth and early nineteenth centuries the burgeoning cotton industry gained notoriety for the exploitation of child labour, to the extent that a Factory Act was passed in 1819 to specifically address this issue. It banned the employment of children under nine, and limited the hours of nine to sixteen year-olds to twelve hours a day, but only in cotton mills. Even so, reports Victor Cohen, its success was limited, due to lack of enforcement. Attempts to improve the children's lot continued to be frustrated, up to and including John Fielden's Act of 1847. Though this in theory limited their working day to ten hours, in practice employers found loopholes. A further Act in 1850 introduced a more enforceable ten-and-a-half hour day, but it was 1853 before the ten hour day, for "children and protected persons" arrived in reality.

It was of course not only in Britain that labour was exploited in the cotton industry. Slavery was abolished by law here in 1833, but until the 1860s the Lancashire cotton industry continued to depend on the import of cotton grown and harvested in America's cotton belt using slave labour. Sculptures in the interior of Dobroyd Castle include the depiction of a slave at work, but Historic England's detailed notes on the building report that, though John Fielden had campaigned against the payment of compensation to former slave owners in Britain, "otherwise there is little evidence regarding the family's attitudes towards slavery."

Spot my camera and tripod in the multi-mirrored stairwell at Dobroyd Castle ►►

◄ *Saw-tooth roof, Woodbottom Mill, Hollins Road, former home of Crossley Shuttles.*

Hollins Mill ▶

Hollins Mill

Hollins Mill, in Walsden, is listed Grade II by Historic England. The listing describes it as an:

> "*Integrated cotton spinning and weaving mill, now mixed uses. 1856-58, extended by 1890. Built by Abraham, William and Peter Ormerod , 'manufacturers from raw cotton to woven fabric for the finisher'.*"

The very detailed official listing also states that the buildings include a 4-storey, 18-bay spinning mill and a single-storey, 25-bay weaving shed; and that the spinning mill contained 30,000 spindles and the weaving shed had 600 looms.

A second, 14 bay, single storey shed, is believed to have been used for "*the preparation processes of unpacking and mixing the cotton, and scutching, the beating process to remove dust and vegetable particles.*"

Seen opposite is the "*saw tooth*" wall of the weaving shed, alongside the Rochdale Road, with part of the spinning mill beyond. Each "tooth" in this wall represents what building surveyors call a bay, and 24 of the 25 listed can be counted here. The saw tooth shape, common in weaving shed walls, arises from the structure of the roof, which in turn arises from the need to maximise the natural light falling on the looms. But this light also needs to be even and free from shadows, so not direct sun. The roof therefore includes north, or in this case, north-west, facing, windows, separated by slate pitches which slope south/south east.

Pam Warhurst presenting apprenticeship ▶
awards for the Forestry Commission

Pam Warhurst, CBE, environmental campaigner.

Pam Warhurst is a people person, and a very busy one. It took me a while to track her down, but eventually we met one Saturday morning in a café on Rochdale Road. I wanted to talk to Pam about *Incredible Edible Todmorden*, but I also knew of her as a former national Chair of both the Forestry Commission and the Countryside Agency. What I did not know, no, really, I didn't, was that Pam was also Chair of the Todmorden Book Festival.

Incredible Edible then: Pam's original idea was of a sustainability and climate change movement, which would get people involved through the power of food: growing food, locally. The most visible evidence of its activity, when you are in Todmorden, is fruit and veg growing here there and everywhere, throughout the town.

Since Pam first sat down to discuss the idea with fellow Todmordener Mary Clear, some ten years ago, *Incredible Edible* has really taken off. More than 120 groups have sprouted in the UK, and in 2018 the *Guardian* reported that there were groups in France, Israel, Palestine, Colombia and Brazil . Prince Charles has been to visit, there is a group in the small town where I live in Mid Wales, and just a week after I met Pam I mentioned Todmorden to a lady from Lincolnshire and she said "*Oh yes, Incredible Edible.*"

Originally from Leigh, now part of Greater Manchester, Pam has lived in Todmorden since the 1970s, initially in Lumbutts. She loves that side of the valley, and loved living in Lumbutts, she says, even when floodwater came in through her back door and out through the front. On the Yorkshire/Lancashire question Pam is diplomatic: "*It takes the best from both,*" she says.

"To the above natural advantages, we must add, the acquired advantage of canal communication, which ramifies itself through all the populous parts of this county, and connects it with the inland counties, the seats of other flourishing manufactures and the sources whence iron, lime, salt, stone and other articles in which Lancashire is deficient, are obtained."

Edward Baines, *History of the Cotton Manufacture*, 1835

The Rochdale Canal

◄ *The Rochdale Canal at Walsden*

The Rochdale Canal passes right through the centre of Todmorden, and it has also played a central rôle in the history of the town. Thirty three miles long, the canal crosses the Pennines to connect Bridgewater Canal in Manchester to the Calder and Hebble Navigation in Sowerby Bridge. It was completed in 1804, and its highest point, between Todmorden and Littleborough, has given a name to both a sizeable community, Summit, and a pub. Also at Summit, Lock Number 37 lays claim to the title of highest broad (as against narrow) lock in England.
Along with much of Britain's canal network, the Rochdale fell out of repair in the 20th century, superseded, first by railways, and later by road transport. Hugh McKnight's 1975 *Shell Book of Inland Waterways* reports that the last boat to travel its full length did so in 1937, and that it was formally "abandoned" by Act of Parliament in 1952.

But even in 1975 a revolution in the nation's attitude to canals, their history, and their future was well under way. The seed for this had been sown by LTC Rolt in his landmark 1944 book, *Narrow Boat*, a lament for the sad state of the nation's waterways and the passing of a water-borne way of life. In the 75 years since *Narrow Boat* there have been numerous restoration schemes, including on the Rochdale. Thousands of people now hire narrow boats for their holidays, and canal towpaths are promoted as long distance walking routes.

◄ The canal's towing path, originally built for horses, passes under the Rochdale road in a gritstone-paved tunnel, and there can indeed be seen Rolt's "grooves worn by the towing lines..... that bring the past to life" . ▼

Forlorn: the Kennet and Avon Canal, in Berkshire, as I found it in 1972. It is now fully restored and navigable. ▶

"There is something indescribably forlorn about these abandoned waterways; like old ruined houses, or silent mills, they are haunted by the bygone life and toil which has left its deathless eloquent mark upon them. Just as in old houses the worn steps are the memorial of many vanished feet, so on the canals it is the grooves worn by the towlines in the rotting wooden lockbeams or the crumbling brickwork of bridges that bring the past to life."

Rolt, *Narrow Boat*, 1944

But of course Britain's canals were originally built for anything but leisure. The Bridgewater Canal, credited with starting the canal boom of the 18th and early 19th century, was opened in 1761, to carry coal from mines at Worsley to markets in Manchester. Welsh slate was carried by canal from Llangollen to London. Village carpenter Walter Rose, writing in 1937, remarks on the novelty of imported softwoods arriving in the English midlands following the construction of the canals.

But in Todmorden it was all about cotton. Raw cotton, imported through Liverpool and Manchester, and manufactured cotton, leaving the town for export all over the world. Cotton and coal for new steam-powered mills which appeared along the canal banks.

All roads lead to Rochdale
The Rochdale Canal, the Rochdale Road, and the railway to Rochdale and Manchester weave over and under each other at Gauxholme. The canal warehouse at bottom right is listed Grade II by Historic England, who record it as late 18th century and having originally contained a "wet-dock." Does it still? At the bottom left can be seen the glass windows of another saw-tooth roof. ▶▶

Death in Todmorden

IN
MEMORY
·OF·
FRED, SON OF EDMUND AND
ELIZABETH SHACKLETON,
OF RAGLAN STREET TODMORDEN,
WHO DIED AUGUST 1ST 1871,
AGED 1 YEAR.
ALSO OF FRANK THEIR SON,
WHO DIED JUNE 17TH 1876,
AGED 1 YEAR AND 7 MONTHS,
ALSO OF EMILY THEIR DAUGHTER,
WHO DIED MARCH 17TH 1881,
AGED 9 MONTHS.
ALSO OF THE ABOVENAMED ELIZABETH
SHACKLETON, WHO DIED JUNE 15TH 1889,
AGED 44 YEARS.

IN MEMORY
SARAH.
DAUGHTER OF
RICHARD & BETTY SUN
OF SPRING-SIDE NET
WHO DIED NOVEMBER
AGED 11 M
ALSO OF JOHN W
WHO DIED JA
AGED
ALSO IT THE
NETHERLAND V

In Loving Memory of
JOHN SUTCLIFFE
OF CHARLESTOWN,
NEAR HEBDEN-BRIDGE,
WHO DIED APRIL 10TH 1891,
AGED 33 YEARS.
ALSO 2 INFANTS,
ALSO OF JOHN EASTWOOD,
OF LOBMILL
BORN OCTOBER 1ST 1853,
DIED FEBRUARY 4TH 188
ALSO OF HANNAH, WIFE OF
ABOVE, WHO DIED DECR

Death stalked the overcrowded industrial towns of northern England in the nineteenth century. Yes, there was disease in the countryside, in rural Buckinghamshire three of my grandfather's four sisters died of TB before the age of 21, but whereas the average life expectancy in Surrey in 1841 was 45, in Manchester two years later it was 24. According to Peter Hall the difference was largely due to "*the shockingly high infant-mortality rates in the northern industrial towns: 259 out of every 1,000 children born died within the first year of life in Liverpool in 1840-41*"

A visit to Cross Stone cemetery, on the northern rim of the Calder valley, brings home some of the human meaning of these cold statistics from long ago. Edmund and Elizabeth Shackelton of Raglan Street lost their son Fred in 1871 at one year of age. Five years later they lost another son at one year and seven months, and in 1881 their daughter Emily died even younger than her two siblings. Elizabeth herself only survived another eight years, dying at 44.

The adjacent grave of John Sutcliffe of Charlestown refers to "2 infants", un-named, and nearby the stone of John Cunliffe, 65, commemorates no fewer than five un-named infants, along with four other adult members of his family. There is nothing to indicate that any of these are buried elsewhere. Are there 5 adults and 5 infants in this one grave?

The story is repeated again and again, with closely-packed headstones featuring long inscriptions to multiple family members. It would seem that it was not only housing for which there was a shortage of land in Todmorden.

In Search of the Quaker Burial Ground

Walking above Todmorden one cold snowy day in 1987 I came across a walled-up gateway, behind which was a small enclosure surrounded by beech trees. The photographs which I took back then suggest a bleak and lonely place. Four flat stone slabs lie on the ground, covered with snow. Another, close by, bears a brief inscription:

HARRIET ODDIE
DIED 6. MO. 16. 1865,
AGED 22 YRS

This is the Quaker, or Friends', Burial Ground.

Twenty six years later I decided to see if I could find it again. I parked my car in Longfield Road with the intention of working my way up the hill on foot to where I thought the burial ground might be. Almost immediately I was distracted when, climbing a flight of steps, I spotted, on the side of a building, an engraved stone bearing the words "*To the memory of Samuel, John, and Joshua Fielden, Constant Benefactors of the Unitarian church and school*". Fieldens! Clearly I could not pass this without taking a photograph.

As I did so I was greeted by a gent emerging from the building, who volunteered the information that the grave of John Fielden, probably Todmorden's most celebrated son, was just around the corner. So, pausing only to photograph an extraordinarily beautiful, and friendly, cat, round the corner I went. And sure enough there in the corner of a small cemetery, right next to the compost heap, was a very plain rectangular plot bearing just the name and dates of John Fielden. It was quite difficult to photograph, and the light was not good, but I had a go.

Next came the Unitarian church, Todmorden's classic example of high Victorian Gothic, highly decorated but also a tad forbidding. As I looked up at the stone spire looming against a heavy sky I'll admit a hint of a shiver ran up my spine. The light was getting still worse but I took a few pictures before pressing on up the hill, still intent on finding the Quaker Burial ground. As I did so I fancied that I heard a rumble of thunder, but this being late October, I dismissed the idea, and concluded that it must have been a heavy lorry on the Rochdale Road, just below.

On up Longfield Road and round a steep double hairpin bend I found another cemetery, this time surrounded by trees and with no obvious building nearby. But this was not the one I was looking for. The rumble came again and I began to think that perhaps it was thunder after all. Onwards and upwards, now on steep tarmac under a leaden sky. As the track levelled off a clump of Beech trees came into view and it seemed that I was nearly there. Sure enough this was the burial ground I had photographed all those years ago. It was very little changed, except that the gateway had been opened up and a rather incongruous plaque in dark Welsh (or perhaps Spanish) slate had been fixed over an earlier inscription carved in local stone. The light now being very poor indeed I had to use my tripod to take a picture of the entrance.

More rumbles and then some flashes in the lowering cloud across the valley. This was definitely a thunderstorm, and it was getting quite near. Through the wrought-iron

gates into the burial ground itself. As I knelt to photograph the gravestones a few drops of rain started to fall. The rumbles of thunder were now more like cracks, and the lightning was getting more frequent. It occurred to me that to be working in a clump of trees on top of a hill in a thunderstorm might be considered by some to be a little unwise. How ironic to be killed by a thunderbolt while photographing a burial ground.

So I hurried along and then packed up my camera bag, closed the gate and set off down the hill again with my tripod over my shoulder. Another flash and crash. I took my tripod off my shoulder. As I passed for a second time the cemetery in the wood the rain seemed to get heavier. By the time I reached the Unitarian Church again it was really raining quite hard. I rounded a corner and suddenly I was back in the town, by the traffic and bustle of the Rochdale road. And there, as my car came into sight, the heavens truly opened. It rained stair-rods, and then ball bearings too. I ran up the hill, threw camera bag and tripod in the boot and leapt into the driver's seat in a deluge of truly, and appropriately, biblical intensity. Hailstones battered at the roof and windscreen as cars passed with headlights on, barely able to see where they were going. Rain was coming down so hard and bouncing up so high that the road surface turned to mist. Everything was awash .

It was truly spectacular, but far too wet for photographs.

clough (klŭf) n. Ravine, steep valley, usu. with torrent bed.
*[OE cloh = OHG klinga, f. Gmc *klanh-]*

Concise Oxford Dictionary

Two Cloughs

◄ *Gritstone bridge and weir in Jumble Hole Clough*

◄ A rather fine arched stone packhorse bridge

Four huge slabs of gritstone with one central pier ▶

Colden Clough

Seeking a photograph of the pre-industrial Pennine landscape described by W.G. Hoskins (p.31), one day I made my way to Blackshawhead, in the hills north east of Todmorden.

A hamlet of gritstone houses among sloping walled fields, Blackshawhead stands below the open moor but, at 340 metres altitude (1,100 ft), well above the deep valley of the River Calder. Here, overlooking Jack Bridge, I found the view on page 30, which seemed to fit the bill. And in that view I spotted, among the fields, cottages and farms, a rather fine arched stone packhorse bridge, which duly became my next destination. Once there I took more photographs, and along came a couple of walkers, who directed me to another interesting bridge, downstream. So down downstream I went.

Sure enough before long I came to a very fine clapper bridge: four huge slabs of gritstone with one central pier. Here there was a steady trickle of walkers passing through, and a quick check of the map showed that both the Pennine Way and Calderdale Way cross the Colden Water here. (I should have already known this, but that's another story.) The Pennine Bridleway is close by as well.

◀ *Abandoned sluice in Colden Clough*

..a small weir, just one course of stone blocks,.. ▶

Then, just below the bridge, I saw a small weir, just one course of stone blocks, a foot or two high, so I took some pictures of that. One thing led to another, and before long I was following the stream deeper and deeper into Colden Clough. There was another, slightly more substantial weir, and a goit led me to a dam which still had some water in. There were various mysterious masonry structures, including a flight of well-worn stone steps, by which I returned to the bank of the stream.

The Clough was now well-wooded, with mature Beech trees, and, while up on the tops it had been a warm sunny day, as I descended the light faded, the temperature dropped and the air became noticeably damp, chilling the skin. Finally I turned to go back, and it was then that I noticed a mist gathering among the trees. It was a little spooky.

Jumble Hole Clough

I have visited Jumble Hole Clough several times, from the 1980s to the present day. It is a fascinating place. In May of 2010 I walked down the clough from Hippins Bridge, south of Blackshawhead. If you do the same you will pass the fine old seventeenth-century stone house of Hippins and then descend into the wooded clough by flights of gritstone steps leading to a modern footbridge over the stream. Here are Bluebells, Bilberry, Meadowsweet and Celandines growing under Sycamore and Silver Birch trees. Beyond the bridge I followed a level path contouring along the south side of the clough. It was of course a mill goit, and I soon came to a depression to the right which looked as though it might have been pond.

Suddenly, beyond a bank of Bilberry, there was Staups Mill. And even though it was the reason for my visit I was still taken aback when it suddenly, silently, loomed up from the floor of the clough. I was actually level with the roof, or where the roof would have been.

I am not the first person to have photographed Staups Mill. Others, including the celebrated landscape photographer Fay Godwin, were there before me. Godwin featured Staups Mill in *Remains of Elmet - A Pennine Sequence*, a book of her photos with poems by the even more celebrated Ted Hughes, a local boy later to become Poet Laureate. The book was published in

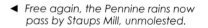

◄ Free again, the Pennine rains now pass by Staups Mill, unmolested.

The mill in 2010 ►

"I like wandering about these lonely, waste and ruined places. There dwells among them a spirit of quiet and gentle melancholy more congenial and akin to my own spirit than full life and gaiety and noise."

Kilvert's Diary, 6th March 1871

1979 and when Godwin took her picture of Staups Mill she managed to include a date stone inscribed "*1812*". Unsurprisingly, comparison of Godwin's 1970s photo, and my 1980s ones, with those which I took in 2010 show a considerable deterioration in the structure. Almost half of the gable end wall disappeared in the intervening years.

So, back on page seven I promised that we would return to Staups Mill. But knowing what we do now, is it really so romantic a ruin? It has a beautiful setting, and there undoubtedly dwells about it the spirit of quiet and gentle melancholy so congenial to Francis Kilvert. This surely is not one of the dark satanic mills of which William Blake wrote in his poem *Jerusalem*. After all, unlike those soot stained, smoke-belching, steam-powered monsters down in the valley, this mill must have been powered by water, pure natural rainwater. What could be less Satanic?

Yet by Victor Cohen's analysis (p.100) this was precisely the kind of isolated and remote location where "*helpless child slaves... were worked as hard a their little bodies would stand*".

A map of 1892 shows Staups Mill as "disused", so it would appear to have been abandoned for more than a century. Should we lament it's crumbling decay? Or celebrate it?

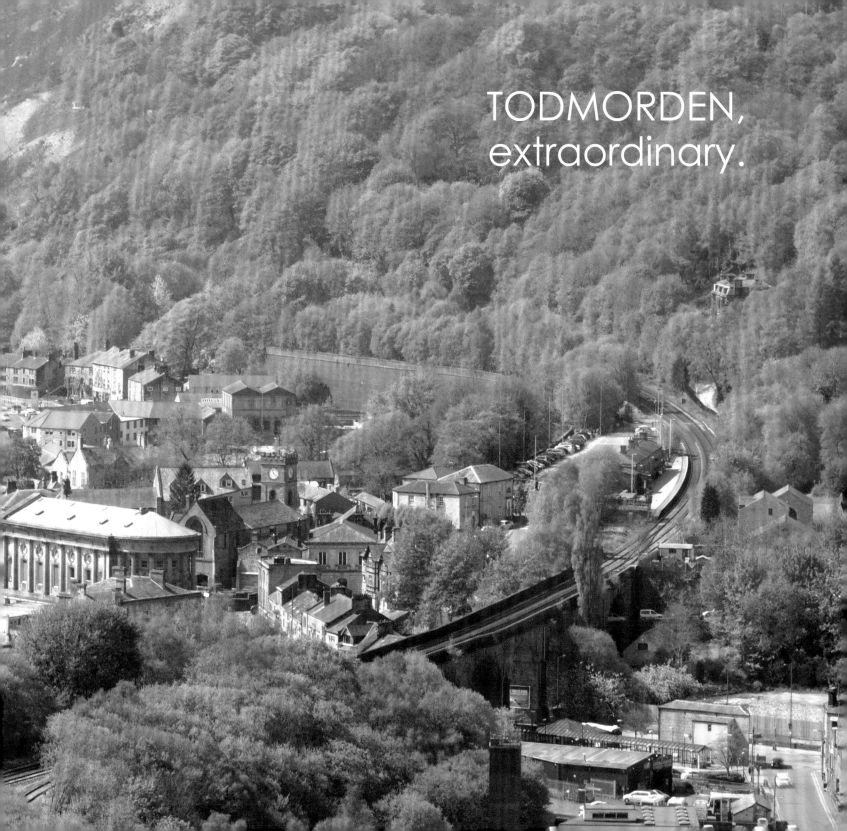

TODMORDEN,
extraordinary.

About the photos.

With the exception of the picture of a cotton plant on page 89, all the photos in this book are my own. Those which date from1974 to1986 were taken on budget Praktica and Fujica 35mm SLRs, but from then onwards I have used exclusively Olympus cameras and lenses, starting with a second-hand OM2 SP. In 1987 I used this, with Ilford Pan F film, to photograph the mill chimney at Pudsey which appears on front the cover, and the Town Hall apse on the back. Later I had a couple of older OM2Ns, and a range of Zuiko prime lenses from 28mm to 300 mm.

In 2005, after careful consideration, I abandoned film in favour of digital photography, but I stayed with Olympus and bought a 5 megapixel Olympus E-1. I found that the results from this compared very favourably with the 35mm Kodachromes which had been my benchmark until then. A couple of years later I blagged a 10 megapixel (10 MP) E-510 direct from Olympus and I have now reached the giddy heights of 20 megapixels with my beautiful little Olympus Pen F.

Though its default output is 20 MP, clever technology enables the Pen F, with stationary subjects, to produce an enormous 80 MP RAW file. This can make a landscape print nearly a metre wide at 300 pixels per inch. All but one of the double-page spreads in this book have been produced by this method.

And finally: all pictures here are of real subjects, as you would have seen them on the day. I have no truck with Photoshop fakery.

Bibliography

An indispensible guide to exploring Todmorden and its hills and cloughs, whether on foot, or from your armchair, is the Ordnance Survey's Explorer Map No. OL21 *South Pennines*.

For a more weighty read here are some of the sources I have consulted in preparing this book:

Baines, Edward *History of the Cotton Manufacture in Great Britain* Fisher, Fisher and Jackson 1835

Batcheldor, Samuel *Introduction and Early Progress of the Cotton Manufacture in the United States...* Little, Brown and Company, 1863. (Available to print-on-demand from University of Michigan Library.)

Chapman, Sydney John *The Lancashire Cotton Industry, A Study in Economic Development* Manchester University Press 1903. Reprinted 2012 by Forgotten Books

Clifton-Taylor, Alec *The Pattern of English Building*, Faber and Faber 1972

Cohen, Victor *The Nineteenth Century - a Biographical History* John Murray 1932

Dixon, Roger, and Muthesius, Stefan *Victorian Architecture* Thames and Hudson 2nd edition 1985

Ekwall, Eilert *The Concise Oxford Dictionary of English Place-Names* Oxford University Press 4th Edition, 1960

Hall, Peter *Urban & Regional Planning* Pelican, 1975

Holden, Joshua *A Short History of Todmorden; With Some Account of the Geology and Natural History of the Neighbourhood*. Manchester University Press 1912. Reprinted 2010 General Books, Memphis, Tennessee (sic)

Hoskins, Prof W.G. *English Landscapes* BBC 1973

McKnight, Hugh *The Shell Book on Inland Waterways*, David & Charles 1975

Raistrick, Arthur *Industrial Archaeology*, Paladin, 1973

True, A.C. *The Cotton Plant- Its History, Botany, Chemistry, Culture, Enemies and Uses* 1896. Re-published by Forgotten Books, 2014.

White, Rev Gilbert *The Natural History of Selborne* First published 1789. My copy by Ward Lock, 1912. New 2013 edition from Oxford University Press.